Poems for Lorca

Walt Shepperd

Published by:
W. D. Hoffstadt & Sons
4451 Cherry Valley Turnpike
Lafayette, NY 13084

Cover design and layout by:
WRKDesigns
Syracuse, NY
www.wrkdesigns.com

Printed in the United States of America

Acknowledgements

Some of these poems appeared in *The Sixties and Beyond, Berkeley Barb, Born into a Felony, Syracuse New Times, Third Voice, Levels, Edcentric, Nitty-Gritty, Nickel Review, Peace News, Jail Ministry, Smoke Signal, Colgate Scene, Gravida, A Window on Experience, Greenfield Review,* and *Intrepid.*

The author makes grateful acknowledgement to all of them.

Contents

For my daughter Lorca

Passing Your House after a Carole King Song
I do not Want to Write Poems for You

I walk past your house
with the lights on
the windows open
a summer stillness
sharpening the memory
of you inside dancing
in your mind bare feet filling
the far corner
of a long leather couch.
I do not want to write
poems for you the muse
must hold aloof pedestaled
beyond production demanding
but I walk past your house
to lessen the distance
and if I hadn't
I would have missed the fireflies.

Umbrella at the Pasta Palace

The umbrella won't go down.

He is a law school graduate.
A judge on a split shift
between here and Brooklyn.
Assessing situations
is his strong suit.
But no matter how much
he fusses with the button
the umbrella won't go down.

The rain has stopped.

He spins it self consciously.
He and his colleague
have approached
the prestigious pasta palace
with the confidence of politicians
running unopposed.

The destination is definitively
desirable.

The DA drops by for take out.
A prominent journalist
can get a hug
from the Congressperson at the bar
or a less effusive greeting
from the mayor.

But doubt is creeping
across the faces of the judge
and his colleague.
No matter how much
he fusses with the button
the umbrella won't go down.

Taking its fully opened space
the umbrella won't fit
through the palace door.

The time for judgement
is at hand.
The judge shows no hesitation
He turns and leads
his colleague
in search of expanded entryway.

His decision is *nolo contendere.*

He Said He Couldn't Wait 'til Judgment Day
for Abbie Hoffman

Our clown prince just died
or maybe just got into bed
with his street clothes on
pulled up the covers
and stopped breathing
to conserve energy
for the next demonstration

or maybe he just levitated himself
into the grandest put-on
human history will ever record
leaving us to wait
for the millennium
or at least the next
decent block party
to determine whether he is
enshrined in the annals of time
as an absolute original
or simply ranked as
another contender
whose finale qualified only
as an admirable near miss

or maybe he got tired
teased too often by curiosity
with the accepted myth
that wearing thorns long enough
guarantees mountains will shake
boulders will move
and rolling stones will gather momentum

or maybe he got bored
with myth and momentum
just got into bed
with his street clothes on
and stopped breathing
because he thought there were
no more cartwheels
left to turn.

An Easement for the Highway in Your Mind

The tinder has dried
and bridges
roots
and the canvas
in the windowframes
of someone else's yesterdays
smolder
from sparks
carried
on an imperceptible breeze
down a road
between
trees
and tents
and tenements
over timbers
charred beyond support
of tomorrow's weight.

They say
you can't go home again
and they are mostly wrong
but your return
must be guided
by bulldozer tracks
and burial mounds
and streams filled in
with silt
of ruins crumbling
from your backward glance.

Sometimes I'd Rather be a Wife

In my darkest of nights
I dream that you
have taken me away from all this
to cook your meals
and wash your clothes
and scrub your kitchen floor.

In my dream you are gone
making waves
on a sea which needs
the special imprint
of your touch.

I wake in the filtered light
and think to
cook
and wash
and scrub for myself
as the window beckons
of uncharted seas.

Sedative

Fire rages
in a yogurt cup
set by the stubbing
of the last cigarette

a distraction

from refugees pausing
on the late night news
to see which way
the war is going.

On Hearing of indictments of the Guards at Kent State

They'll kill us, you know
and wait to dull
the romance of the barricades
and then they'll punish
somebody
so our parents won!t be mad we died.

But parents too
live out their lives
and those of us without concern
for our golden years
are rapidly losing our cover.

This Place

This place is faces
out of place
faces waiting
to move from one place
to another place
faces hoping
to be placed
on lists
allowing them time
in a better place,
faces out of place
knowing the need
to be someplace else.

The Hubs

Waiting under the overpass
in case it rains to talk
of where the jobs are and
no where waiting for someone
you know or even don't
know as long as they might
have a quarter to get you
across the street and in
the door and out again
with something to share
and talk about where the
jobs are and nowhere
under the overpass
in case it rains.

A Poem for Them, for Us, for You, But Mostly for Me

Freedom is a precious thing
preserved by only constant choice
of what we do
and who we!re with
and how
and why
and all those things
that used to be
proscribed
by The Manfs Law.

A friend reminded me
that once there was a blackbird
afraid to fly   (don't need the sky)
afraid of rain   (I don't dig pain)
afraid to soar   (might want some more)
afraid to split   (I might get hit)
afraid that all the other birds
were simply playing games with words.

And then one day his house burned down.

An inner voice just told him, Wow!
but other voices said, Look now
look here
the time is gone for all that fear.

We'll pick you up, and we'll let go
your wings
and it will show
that flying gives off its own glow.

And, oh yes, you should know
that free birds aren't always alone
you'll see
we can fly together
and still stay free.

Power to the People

Last night someone stayed out late
painting slogans on the sidewalk.
At the Street Cleaning Department
the workers are oppressed.
Their consciousness has not been raised.
They are angry.
They cannot clean the paint
up off the sidewalk.

The Balladeer

Four more songs
'til a break,
a chance to drink
the edge off the boredom
standing always moving
hiding wrinkles from the spot light
moving quickly
to hide another year
etched on his face
since the last time
he played this club.

Four more, of the same songs
now like breathing
mechanical like a stereo
with human parts
and four more songs
before something
inside him
clicks off.

What You Started Tomorrow
They Had Already Finished Today
for Patricia Soltysik

You must have found some peace by now
a place to rest
and watch the seasons change
away from running
and the fire
that seared your brain
like the flames
that charred your flesh.

A poet called you
Mizmoon
was it from a Joplin song
you heard that sparkling first prom night
while flames burned huts
and scorched the brick of tenements?
Did you dance
while children died
and later learn regret?

We watched you dying
in the flames
behind the smoke
that masked your fear
your driving hate
your love for those
who shook their heads
and knew the object
of your lesson plan
before you knew yourself.

Our teachers all are quiet now
they showed us what we couldn't be
they showed us where we couldn't look
in our search
for the new land
where flames of campfires
cast strobe-like shadows
of a dance to love
and the promise of tomorrow.

Tomorrow came
and you weren't there
those hundred whistles
to your one
did not invite you to the dance
and those you loved
still shake their heads
they share your fear
your hate
your love
but they want to watch the seasons change
they are looking
for another way.

A Window on Experience

Lock the door behind you
and enter a cavern
now a treadmill
now a stage
now a ramp for wind-up walkers
careening
off the walls
and the sky
and each other.

Lock the door behind you
and let the key slide
into fingers just beyond your grasp
through a gate
on the frame
of a window on experience.

Lock the door behind you
as the day begins
with the coming of sleep
and ends as you wake
but lock the door behind you
this time it's all real.

8:07AM, Draper, Utah
for Gary Gilmore

You gave people little choice
compelling themselves into your life
compelling others
compelling decision appeals
waiting games
time to sense the pulse of apathy
and all you wanted to do was die
quick.

What was so compelling
about your life?

The first execution in ten years
an ultimate test
of the services provided
by the system in which you grew
organs divided up to save
the lives of others
with dignity, your uncle said
"bing, bing, bing,"
your bearded literary agent
described the shots
"If there was a fourth it overlapped."

And that same day
in the afternoon sun
of a Dublin tenement courtyard
a lion broken free
from a passing circus
basked
for two hours
before reluctantly returning
to his cage.

For Your Consideration

If I could infiltrate
a corner of your consciousness
I would ask you to consider
what it must be like
to be locked away without knowing
whether children in their private thoughts
still giggle with that special tone
or sleep expressionless
in the calm of restful innocence
to be locked away without knowing
whether love can last
when nurtured only through
fingertips across a crowded table
or the length
of a two page letter form
to be locked away without knowing
whether prayers are heard
by anyone
when the only certainty
is that of being locked away
without knowing.

Changing Faces
for Brian Bourke

Watching late night snow
frosting the pumpkin
before Autumn fully changes face
we shudder at the sudden chill
thoughts of things gone early
he, with boy scout countenance
always the last to leave the set
lest he miss a twitch
in the changing face of culture
gone early
a voice we took for granted
giving us meaning for
what we thought we might have heard
for the moment
or forever.

Forever's bill came due
on those who have already overpaid
a decision without appeal
with meaning lost
like the early frost
limiting the pumpkin's possibility
in the changing face of immediacy.
We see the frost and feel the chill
watch the set and sense the absence.

He is gone early
reminding us
if you love someone
tell them today
in the changing face of reality
they may not be here tomorrow.

Take a Memo to Diogenes

Seeking
ten years and more
of seeking
searching
back alleys and basketball courts
ballot boxes
sensual sanitariums
and steamy storefront windows
seeking
the teachers of our generation
who bred a sense of discontent
who sat at desks
and waited for despair
who walked the streets in panic
who spoke of building barricades
at vined down week-end seminars
who talked of guns
but had no time for target practice
who formulated power
from headlined hiding places
who sat in waves
of tear gas clouds
chanting mantras
to a world of love
between those
seeking
the simplicity of right and those
who wanted simply
to be left alone
with the truth
in the eyes
of a six year old
as she buries her kitten
who has died.

Happy, Happy Birthday, Critic

I am 30 years old
and have holes in my shoes
on the sides
where the puddles surge in
as I walk home
from a concert
which I'll write about.
They'll pay me ten bucks.

Everyone enjoyed the concert
except me.

If I don't find
something wrong with it
they won't pay me ten bucks.

Basketball Jones, Baby, Oooh Weee Oooh
for the Lady Wessex

At your best you respond
when you had no idea
a game had been scheduled
when the horn sounds
hushing the crowd
a voice asserting itself
announcing tournament time
announcing this is not a game.

You are a tournament player
in semi-retirement
your trophy case crowded
and gathering dust
you have maintained
the ritual of working out
the rhythm of practice
in solitude
playing through the pain
comfort in the knowledge
you have been ready
for more opening horns
than any crowd expected
especially the ones
those scheduling the match
intended only
to send you home
in a body bag.

You have burned your scrapbook
full of frozen images
poses of awkward seriousness
fading numbers indicating only
that there was a score
and someone else's judgement
on how you played the game.

The Voice
hums into the night
there is no clock
ticking to a final buzzer
the points scored
count for both
in a match of minds
merged in graceful ballet
for a tournament
without elimination.

Easter Morning News

Races are most safely run
in circles getting you back
to somewhere you've been
so that at the end
if you've lost
at least you have
familiar turf to remind
you who you are.

I have been running
in an outside lane
with too much ground
to make up outside
seeing too many headlines
telling too many endings
to a story no one should
have started.

It is cold in the outside lane –
the FBI says that after all
some parents do kill their
own children – the outside
lane loses too much ground,
it is time to cross over
to the inside track.

Suburban Park

Once it brought your stomach
all the way up
into your mouth
or stuffed it with junk
in between rounds
of screams and dizziness.

Once it accepted
coins in slots
for flashing lights
and ringing bells
punctuating the rush
or wheels on rails,
steamed notes from the carousel
or the organ's call
to a skater's waltz.

Now, overgrown with weeds
signs sold off for souvenirs,
the wind plays music
through the rusted hulk
of a fun machine.

Rate of Exchange

I don't smoke
when I work in a prison.

Cigarettes are money
in prison
and if you use nicotine
to stay in touch with yourself
& not lose all reason
in the eye of a hurricane
swirling away every shred
of all your current realities,
then you will find yourself
chain smoking.

If you sit and burn money
the whole time they see you
the inmates will think you rich
and resent,
more than usual,
what they perceive to be
your freedom.

Dear Dad, If They Have a Nuclear War Please Pick Me Up Early from School

Dear Dad,
If they have a nuclear war
Please pick me up early from school
so we can pick mom up from work
and we can go get fast food and I promise
I'll eat my salad and we can go
to the movies 'cause teacher made
us stand in line to learn about
nuclear war and said look at
the person next to you they'll
be dead Johnny was next to me
and his birthday party is next week
if they have a nuclear war and
Johnny's dead can I still go
to his party and before you
pick me up early from school
make a bomb shelter for my
gerbil in the microwave oven
so we can pick mom up from work
and get fast food and we can
go to the movies and go up
high in the back where the movie
comes from and find a space ship
and go be safe and I promise
I'll eat all my salad.

For Melvin, In Case You Die

First son bred
for the manor born
to inherit everything
regardless of merit
competence
or inclination.
Second son
to the military
to prove himself
be blooded
and rise to occasions
of restlessness
when natives required
reminder of their place.
Third son to the clergy
if survival smiled
completing the equation
requisite for maintaining
the civilization we were
tutored to accept.

History played a trick on us.

It was hard to imagine
you a native
first brother to the post office
second to the steel mill
third to jail and the asylum
while you avoided restlessness
reading Sartre and Camus
in the dusk
of a ghetto playground.

We encountered each other
that first day at dinner
without expectation beyond
the shared obsessions
of basketball
shooting pool
late night card games
unreconstructed rhythm and blues
and the preciseness of civilized language.

I wondered how
you could be so polite
with the drunken sons
of colonial masters
who begged you
to dance at their parties
and win the school glory
while throwing bottles
as you walked to practice
down fraternity row
and you wondered why
I rushed to embrace
those uncivilized words
and let the silver spoon slip
so thoughtlessly
through my grasp.

Your persistence won you
a seat by power's door
a title as master of words
on the daily record of empire's decline
and at your peak
you left it
with little more to prove.

Now you have left me
blooded
my silver spoon passing
to the next generation
fumbling with equations
our mentors warned us against.

I will miss you
in the dusky ghetto playgrounds.

Your strength is my inheritance.

Winter (Yet to Come)

The Winter will come, and be bad
so bad Rockefeller Center skaters rip blades from their shoes
so bad Arctic Explorers pack no food for returns
so bad there will be no children
so bad Human Rights Commissions will be flooded
with complaints about the Hawk
and the flood will freeze
and it'll be worse than that, even
so bad very few will say
"I told you it would be this bad"
and fewer still
"It could have been worse."

They will tell us it is far from over
and form a Karma Squad
cruising the nation
zapping those whose Karma lags
subtracting Karma points
growing old past their wisdom
devoured on icecaps by polar bears.

And when they've subtracted points from everyone
you and I will remember the Spring.

I Dreamt I Took a Two Week Vacation in an Audrey Hepburn Movie

I never wanted birthdays
and Christmas
and mother's day
to be what now
it seems
they must become,
excuses for remembering
that time is now a luxury.

We build new worlds
and gather things
that patch the strands
that chafe our shells
that brace our memories
into barricades
that must stand by themselves,
for time is now a luxury.

The things we gather
gather dust
the barricades
won't stand a charge
the boxes burn
the seeds grow mold
the papers crumble in the light,
and love becomes the luxury.

Survey

If you tell ten people you love them
at what seem to be appropriate times,
and one throws up
and two say thank you
and one puts you on hold
and three reply impatiently
that they already knew
and the rest stare dumbly
with undecided eyes
then your emotions test out randomly
and the margin for error
significantly diminishes.

A Rainy Day is Like Looking for Work

A rainy day is like
looking for work
passing grey merged faces
like waste passed unconsciously
concentrating on the captions in PEOPLE Magazine
faces passing grey promising
uncertain futures telling people
I can get my own coffee
do my own typing
answer my own phone
to whatever harassment
and I'm sorry this shreds your job description
but here's a chance to be creative
what was it you wanted to do with your life
reflected in a resume
read by some remarking
it looks like you have a hard time
holding a job.

Yesterday the sun remembered
the birds sang early
the dark came late
for one psychic moment
a universe in cosmic balance
and me looking for work.

Journalist's Prayer

This here's final copy, Lord.
You might find a whole lot of extra words
which I probably wouldn't ordinarily use,
but I got this deadline, Lord,
and I want to get some sleep tonight.

Grant me absolution for misspelling, Lord.
Forgive me those facts I never really checked out.
But watch my style, Lord,
you know my style,
and if I blow it
return my carriage all the way with a lightning bolt
but ring a bell first so I can run
one last poem before they clean my desk.

And if that really happens, Lord,
with the lightning bolt and all,
do me a favor Lord
call the wire services.
There's an obituary in my top drawer.

About Walt Shepperd

Walt Shepperd has read poetry at colleges and cultural centers throughout Central New York as well as New York City's Lincoln Center, City Center, Nuyorican Cafe, and the Poetential Unlimited Theater of Harlem. With Stewart Brisby, on a grant from the National Endowment for the Arts, he edited and published *Born into a Felony*, the first national anthology of contemporary American prison writing.

Mr. Shepperd is Executive Producer for the *Media Unit* and Senior Editor at *UrbanCNY*. He is a three-time winner of the New York Press Association Writer of the Year Award and a recipient of the Syracuse Press Club Lifetime Achievement Award.

A graduate of Colgate University, with graduate work at Syracuse University's Maxwell School, he has served on the faculties of Colgate, SU, Onondaga Community College, Madison Jr. High, EOC at Jamesville Penitentiary, and the maximum security prisons at Auburn and Attica where he conducted poetry workshops.

He served for eight years as a panelist on Time Warner Cable's Reporters Roundtable. For three decades, his Media Unit's Rough Times Live teen-produced weekly television program has been broadcast in Syracuse, Binghamton, Ithaca, Rochester, and New York City. It has been cited with the Golden Mic Award as "America's Best Local Television Program in the Interest of Youth," and three New York State Golden Mics.

A recipient of the New York Civil Liberties Kharas Award, Shepperd received a Golden Apple Award from the New York Teacher's Association for educational reporting and an Impartial Citizen Award for reporting on race relations. Past President of the Syracuse Press Club and past President of the Cultural Resources Council Board of Directors, he has served on the boards of the Central New York State chapter of the National Organization for Women, the Westcott Youth Organization and the Equal Opportunity Center, the advisory board for the Great New York State Fair, and the Mayor's advisory board on cable television.

Author of *Conjuring a Counter-Culture, Essays on the Sixties*, and *I Dreamt I took a Two Week Vacation in an Audrey Hepburn Movie*, a chapbook of poems, he is Associate Editor on *Chris Powell's Home Town News*, founding editor and publisher of *Nickel Review*, founding editor of the *Syracuse Gazette*, and Senior Editor for 35 years at the *Syracuse New Times*. Shepperd's work has also been published in the *Berkley Barb, Newsday*, the *Post-Standard, Scholastic Teacher* and *HomeFurnishings Daily*. His weekly column appears in *The Syracuse Eagle*.